FROM **FRUIT** TO JELLY

by Shannon Zemlicka

Lerner Publications Company / Minneapolis

Lerner Publications Company
A division of Lerner Publishing Group, Inc.
241 First Avenue North
Minneapolis, MN 55401 U.S.A.

Website address: www.lernerbooks.com

Library of Congress Cataloging-in-Publication Data

Zemlicka, Shannon.
    From fruit to jelly / by Shannon Zemlicka.
      p.   cm. — (Start to finish)
    Summary: An introduction to the process of making jelly, from the time the farmer plants a bush or tree to the time someone eats a peanut butter and jelly sandwich.
    ISBN-13: 978-0-8225-0942-4 (lib. bdg. : alk. paper)
    ISBN-10: 0-8225-0942-3 (lib. bdg. : alk. paper)
    1. Jelly—Juvenile literature. [1. Jelly.] I. Title. II. Start to finish (Minneapolis, Minn.)
TX612.J4 Z46 2004
641.8'52—dc21   2002014355

Manufactured in the United States of America
2 3 4 5 6 7 – DP – 13 12 11 10 09 08

The photographs in this book appear courtesy of: © Royalty-Free/CORBIS, cover; © Todd Strand/ Independent Picture Service, pp. 1 (both), 3, 11, 13, 15, 23; © Robert Holmes/AGStockUSA, p. 5; © Keith Seaman/AGStockUSA, p. 7; © Erin Liddell/ Independent Picture Service, pp. 9, 17, 19, 21.

Special thanks to Minnestalgia for their help with the photographs in this book.

Table of Contents

Jelly is a great snack!

How is it made?

A farmer grows fruit plants.

Jelly starts as fruit. Most of the fruit used for making jelly grows on farms. This farmer is growing plum trees.

The fruit grows.

Flowers bloom on the plum trees in the spring. The flowers grow into plums. The fruit grows all summer.

Workers pick the fruit.

The farmer checks the fruit as it grows. Workers pick the fruit when it is the right size and color for making jelly. Trucks take the fruit to a **factory.** A factory is a place where things are made.

9

The fruit is crushed.

The fruit is washed and put in a steel pot called a **vat.** The fruit is crushed. Juice flows out of the crushed fruit.

The juice is heated.

The fruit juice may contain **germs.** Germs are tiny living things that can make people sick. The juice is heated to kill the germs. Then it is safe for making jelly.

Workers add sugar and pectin.

Workers stir sugar into the juice so that the jelly will taste as sweet as it should. A powder called pectin is added. Pectin is needed to help the juice thicken into jelly.

The mixture is heated again.

The juice, sugar, and pectin are heated. The mixture becomes so hot that it begins to bubble. It is **boiling.**

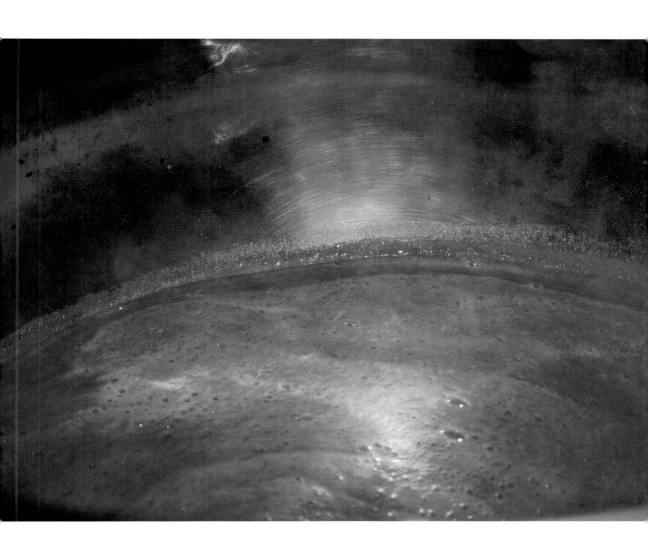

The mixture is put in jars.

The boiled juice mixture is poured into jars. It cools. The pectin makes the juice very thick. The juice becomes jelly.

The jelly is sent to stores.

The jars of jelly are packed into boxes. Trucks take the boxes to stores. Shoppers buy jars of jelly and take them home to eat.

Please pass the jelly!

The farmer's fruit has become jelly. Let's have jelly on toast. Do you like strawberry, plum or grape?

Glossary

boiling (BOY-ling): bubbling from being heated

factory (FAK-tuhr-ee): a place where things are made

germs (JUHRMZ): tiny living things that can make people sick

pectin (PEK-tihn): a liquid or powder that makes juice thicken

vat (VAT): a big steel pot

Index